Santa Claus

A BOOK ABOUT SANTA AND HIS ELVES AT MOUNT KORVATUNTURI, FINLAND

BY MAURI KUNNAS

with Tarja Kunnas
Translated by Tim Steffa

OTAVA PUBLISHING COMPANY · HELSINKI

Far, far away in Finnish Lapland, in a world of northern lights and sunless winters, surrounded by trackless wilds, rises Mount Korvatunturi. On the slopes of this mountain there is a curious village, with houses, workshops and stables. It even has its own airfield.

So far away from human habitation is this village
that no one is known to have seen it, except for
a couple of old Lapps who stumbled across it by
accident on their travels. Few believed their stories
though.

Who on earth would want to build a village
in such a place?

Well, who else but Santa Claus?

This is where every child's very own Santa Claus lives. A kind old gent with a white beard, he toils year in and year out to give us all a merry Christmas. Santa lives at Korvatunturi with his elderly wife, surrounded by hundreds of elves and reindeer.
No one can remeber how Santa came to Korvatunturi, or where he came from. And it's no use asking the old man himself. He just smiles and is silent. Perhaps he himself no longer remembers …

It is said that the other elves are former guardian spirits of households and forests who, over the years, fled from the modern cities and industry of the south to the peace and quiet of Korvatunturi.

The old elves and their wives are skillful folk. Their job is to make Christmas gifts for all good children, and so they represent many different trades: there are carpenters, cobblers, precision mechanics, painters, weavers, printers and many, many others.

They work diligently all year long, from January to December. There's a great deal to remember and arrange, but in his office Santa has good bookkeepers and other enthusiastic helpers.

Life at Korvatunturi is a hive of activity. Every morning the elfin menfolk wake to the mouth-watering aroma of porridge. The bearded old gents are up in a flash and scurrying to the breakfast table. You see, no one wants to miss out on Mrs. Claus's delicious porridge – though there's little chance of that, since it's prepared by the huge potful.

Their bellies bulging, the elfin codgers begin their work-filled day.

Mrs. Claus and the elves' wives certainly have their hands full, what with all the cleaning, cooking, baking, and feeding of all the animals, large and small, at Korvatunturi. There is also a good deal of darning, laundering and patching to do, for anything can happen during the working day. One elf might nail his coat to a workbench, another might pour glue in his pocket.

There's a wonderful community spirit among the folks of Korvatunturi. That's why so many wild animals come and spend their winters under Santa's protection.

After a hard day's work, everyone gradually prepares for bed. The weariest elves fall asleep right after their evening bath, while others have an evening snack or read a few pages from a book.

Elves don't need much space. They're contented with a bed of their own and room for a few favorite things. It all makes for a bit of a jumble, according to Mrs. Claus, but that doesn't bother the elves. On the contrary, they consider it quite cosy.

Arthur, who was once a stable elf in the
south, has tried sleeping between sheets,
but for him nothing can beat the fragrance
and comfort of a haystack.

Elfin children attend school just like human boys and girls. They too learn to read, write, sing, count and draw.

Zoology is the favorite subject of most elfin children. It's little wonder, since the animals at Korvatunturi are so tame that, if you liked, you could even look into a wolf's mouth and count its teeth.

The teacher is very strict about mastering the geography lessons. After all, every elf has to know where Austria, Iceland, Copenhagen and Cologne are.

Elfin children must know many more crafts than human children do, and their teachers are genuine masters of these crafts. The best work done in school often finds its way into Santa's bag of gifts.

Sometimes the herder elves climb up to spend the night in the sheds in which the Lapps store their provisions, out of reach of wild animals.

Santa's reindeer wander the nearby slopes, browsing on lichen. The job of herding the reindeer naturally falls to the former forest elves and their offspring, since they're used to living out-of-doors. They enjoy their work among the gentle, obedient reindeer very much and, what is more, they have excellent reindeer-herding dogs to help them.

Many workshop elves would be glad to trade places with the herders, particularly in the autumn, when the hills are cloaked in brilliant colors and the little elves in their red caps are barely visible amidst the foliage.

Each of Santa's rendeer wears a tiny tinkling bell on its ear. That makes it easy to identify, so the Lapps know at once if one of Santa's reindeer has strayed into their herds.

There are dozens of different workshops at Korvatunturi: a carpenters's, a painter's, a weaver's, a potter's, and many more …
There's quite a racket in the carpenter's workshop.

WATCH YOUR FINGERS

Saws whine, hammers bang, lathes hum, drills buzz and sawdust flies as the elves make presents for children. With their deft hands they can make anything, from wooden beads to baseball bats.

But special care must be exercised in the workshop, for some of the machines there aren't what you'd call harmless.

At the Korvatunturi printing works all sorts of paper things, such as books, games and writing pads, are printed on an enormous press.

The other Korvatunturi elves are amused by the printer elves' black fingers and, in particular, by their funny way of braiding their beards or tying them up on top of their heads. But this isn't just some fashion craze. You see, a long beard can easily get caught in the rollers of the press or dipped in an ink vat.

The work at Korvatunturi procedes like clockwork. Charlie Chisel is a master turner, while Sam Screwdriver is the fastest fastener of skate blades in the village.

Mick the Elf knows all the tricks of the mechanic's trade.

Old Toby Gluebeard is a skilled gluer. How do you think he got his outrageous name?

A brand new doll needs lots of new clothes. That means considerable work for Lind Linen.

Aaron bores holes in horns.

Everyone had best keep their distance when Old Mother Squirt is at work with her spray gun.

The wares are taken from the workshops to huge storerooms. Crates of car wheels, dolls' feet and all sorts of mysterious toy parts are stored there. But as the year goes on, more and more finished articles begin to appear on the shelves.

Making sure that there are enough of each sort of pram and teddy bear keeps the warehouse elves more than occupied.

The little elves are chased out of the toy storerooms during busy working hours. The warehouses are so irresistible that, if the weren't off limits, they would soon be full of romping elfin small fry. How could anyone do any work?

But the elves' life isn't all work and no play, of course. They have regular vacations every summer. There's more spare time then anyway, perhaps because the sun doesn't set at all.

   The elves then hike around on the mountain, play croquet, paint porcelain and practice their synchronized swimming. Korvatunturi even boasts a fine brass band, which is renowned, at least, for its enthusiasm.

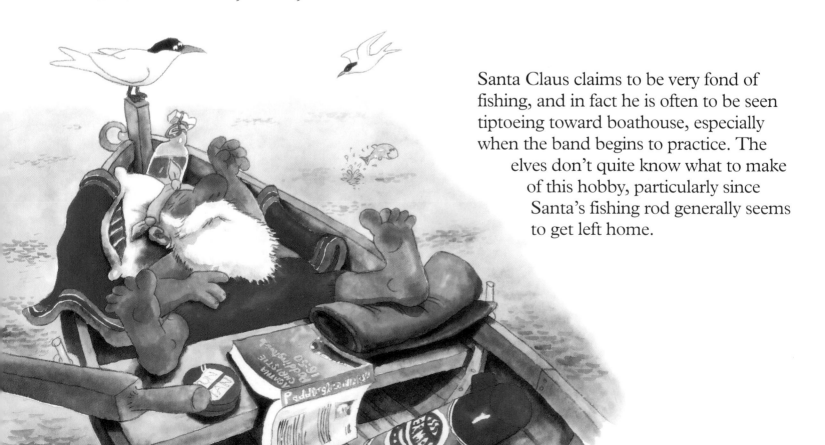

Santa Claus claims to be very fond of fishing, and in fact he is often to be seen tiptoeing toward boathouse, especially when the band begins to practice. The elves don't quite know what to make of this hobby, particularly since Santa's fishing rod generally seems to get left home.

Lately the theater has been the most popular pastime among the elves. It's no wonder, for Paul, the leader and director of the Drama Club, was once the guardian spirit of the National Theater.

In late autumn Santa Claus sends out his scouting patrols. The quickest, smallest and quietest elves are chosen for this demanding task, for elf scouts must travel and operate unseen. These are the elves who observe children from hiding and keep notes on what they see. There's good reason, just before the Christmas season, to brush your teeth regularly, do your homework, go to bed when you're told, help your mother, and be polite to everyone. You never know but what a tiny elf might be hiding somewhere near.

Nothing gives Santa more pleasure
than to have the elves return from
their scouting expeditions
with good news.

Before long, letters start arriving in huge numbers at Korvatunturi.
There are no roads to Santa's village, but an aeroplace from the
General Post Office brings the mail to Korvatunturi by special
delivery.

All of the letters are read, and each child's wishes are recorded in a huge book.

The elf scribes have to know quite a few languages, for they receive letters from dozens of countries. Sometimes, though, the little writers make spelling mistakes. But the scribes have managed all right so far, for only now and then have they had to ask the professors at the University of Helsinki about a word or two.

Of course, amid all the hustle and bustle, the elves prepare for their own Christmas as well.

Willie Whittle makes Christmas decorations enough for Korvatunturi too. Other decorations are made of straw.

And there are sheaves of grain for the little birds.

A huge pot of rice pudding is prepared. Who will find the goodluck almond in their bowl this year?

The baking of Christmas pastries and gingerbread is the high point of the little elves' Yuletide preparations. They get out of school for this. Although two days are spent baking vast amounts of all sorts of treats, there are never enough. That's because the old elfin gents are so wild about sweets.

The wrapping of the gifts is a great event, and everyone at Korvatunturi takes part. There is singing of Christmas carols, and cheerful chatter fills the rooms. There is a steady flow of toys from the brimming storerooms to the wrapping tables.

The elves consult the great books to find out which sorts of presents are to go to each child this year. In the end the place is so full of colorful packages that it's all the elves can do to find their way around among them.

Nowadays parents buy most of their children's presents. After all, with so many children in the world making so many wishes, it would be impossible for Santa to grant them all. But every child also gets something from Korvatunturi. Santa Claus never forgets anyone.

It is only a few days to Christmas now. The sleighs and sleds are brought out, the reindeer harnesses are made ready, and the sleighbells are polished. Santa's and the elves' best suits are brought down from the attic and brushed.

The aeroplanes (without which Santa couldn't possibly manage these days) are serviced and fueled, and the loading of the presents begins.

The overseas packages go into the first and second planes, the presents to southern climes into the third plane, and the fourth carries its cargo all the way to Australia.

Finally the big day arrives – it's Christmas Eve. Everyone gets up at five o'clock. They all have a hearty breakfast of porridge and dress in their warm underwear and finest clothes. Each elf knows his duties and where he should be.

There is a final to see that the compasses and maps in every sleigh are in order, and that the provisions have not been overlooked. Some strong liniment must be rubbed on Santa's back, for a whole day's ride in a cold sleigh is no laughing matter for a man of his years.

It's always a wonderful site to see them set out in the early morning, illuminated by the northern lights.

Christmas Eve is
a time of excitement
and expectation.
Santa's crew is on
its way, but no one
knows when or where
they will appear.
Anyone outside
in the dim light is
mistaken for either
a reindeer or an elf.

At last the familiar knocking and jingling sound on the porch.
»Are there any good children in this household?« Santa asks, knowingfull well
the answer.
But Santa can't stay long, for there are many homes to visit and only one
evening to do it in.

The elves' journey continues and, whether the recipient happens to be on land or at sea, even the smallest of packages is delivered to the correct address.

»The great wide world is sure different from Korvatunturi,» the elves reflect. »So many beautiful houses and cities. People may live in different sorts of houses and landscapes, and even have different customs, but children are the same everywhere.»

Christmas Eve turns to night before Santa Claus and his elves arrive in the lands beyond the sea. The children and adults there are already asleep behind closed doors. But the custom here is for Santa's elves to enter the houses through the chimneys.

They leave the presents in stockings hung from the mantelpiece or place them under the Christmas tree for the families to discover when they wake up in the morning. Of course, by that time there's not a trace left of the elves, except perhaps the odd lump of snow tracked in on their shoes.

The countless number of homes calls for the emptying of many thermoses of juice and coffee before they have all been visited. How on earth does Santa get around to so many places? Even the oldest and wisest Korvatunturi elves can't fathom it, nor has Santa ever explained it to them. »It's the magic of Christmas,» he says with a smile.

Their task completed, the weary but happy travellers return to Korvatunturi. And what could be better than the hot sauna the folks at home have prepared for them? The old elves are too tired to discuss the evening's events, but after all they do have an entire year to talk them over.

The reindeer aren't forgotten either. Their harnesses are removed, they are curried and covered with blankets in their snug stables. They certainly have earned their meal of lichen and a good rest.

Everyone is contented. Another Christmas has passed, with a happy ending. With the joyful laughter of thousands of children echoing in the elves's ears, the Sandman takes charge, and the bearded old gents are soon fast asleep.

The labors of the previous day are over, and on Christmas morning the elves are up and on their way to church. After that they sit reverently and watch the Christmas pageant performed by the little elves in the school assembly room.

Christmas at Korvatunturi
would not be complete without
a few small Christmas presents.
But for the elves it's not the
number of gifts that matters.
What counts is that they are
given from the heart.

Finally, Santa Claus and all the folk of Korvatunturi, from the biggest to the smallest, gather for their own Christmas celebration. A large tree stands in the middle of the straw-covered floor. The elves and their wives eat their tasty Christmas pudding, and everyone waits with bated breath to see whose bowl the almond turns up in this year.

Carols are sung and games are played around the Christmas tree. The children admire their gifts, and the merriment rises to the rafters. Peals of laughter ring out, and the revelry continues well into the night, until one elf after another grows tired and falls asleep. It will be several weeks before Korvatunturi awakens, returns to normal, and begins to prepare for the next Christmas.

The fifth edition

Translated by Tim Steffa
Copyright © 1981 by Mauri and Tarja Kunnas
The original Finnish title Joulupukki published
by Otava Publishing Company Ltd. 1981
Printed in Finland by Otava Book Printing Ltd. 2005

ISBN 951-1-17754-0